Georgilia Cormoş

•

Connected

From 0 to ∞

Georgilia Cormoş holds a bachelor's in psychology and one in translation from Babes-Bolyai University, Cluj-Napoca. She is fluent in 6 languages and this ability has provided her the opportunity to work with people all over the world, expanding her knowledge and understanding.

With an experience of over a decade of publishing articles in several magazines and blogs, she is a freelance mentor who works with kids and adults at the intersection of personal and relationships transformation.

During the pandemic she has taken the opportunity to study several online courses on life coaching, positive psychology and early years education.

Georgilia Cormoş

Connected

From 0 to ∞

2024

Acknowledgments

To my brothers Gratian and Bogdan for their valuable support.

To Tiberius for teaching me important lessons during our 12 years together.

CUPRINS

Foreword

This book is for the people of any age who want to create conscious, fulfilling relationships. You can wish a lifetime for a meaningful relationship, but unless you do something to create it, you will have to live with the hope.

Many people are still not aware about the impact the romantic relationships have on their life. Choosing a partner to share your life with is one of the most important decisions you take in your life.

When we are young, we can easily fall in love, dismissing the essence to the appearance, without further thinking about consequences. Then we may wake up ten, fifteen or twenty years later feeling stuck and uncertain about how to move forward.

Choosing the right partner early in life can save you from years of stress, mental health issues and potential wounds and traumas you would have experienced with the wrong person. More than this, if you were involved in a toxic relationship, it is very likely that you would pass some of your wounds to the future generations, perpetuating the dysfunctional circle. Also, there are numerous studies that show how stress and anxiety deteriorate not only our mental health, but our physical health too.

Although one can never predict the future, you can increase your chances for a better one if you act with awareness, responsibility and ownership. Building a conscious relationship is not a destination to be reached, but a journey to be enjoyed.

My approach suggests going on the relationship journey by discovering yourself first, then aligning your intentions with actions to find and get to know a potential partner, and, ultimately, to consciously create the relationship you want by educating yourself regarding the threats a relationship may pose (becoming toxic, handling conflict etc.) and regarding the essential requirements for a relationship to thrive (acceptance, authenticity, autonomy).

In the end, I want you to become aware about the fact that 'happily ever after' is something that we have the power to create and cocreate in our relationships.

The objective of this book is to guide you to be able to establish a true, authentic connection from the point zero, the moment you are about to start a relationship, to infinity, the moment when the connection created is deep, unlimited and nobody can take it away from you.

I believe everyone deserves a relationship where it feels safe to share your wounds, voice your doubts, be honoured for who you are and hold space for your emotions.

In the infinite connection, you have the ability to metabolize what could be considered a threat and see your relationship as a teacher that life brings you to transform, change and grow.

This is the power of the infinite connection, of being spontaneous, of living in the 'here and now' and having the best experiences as long as they last. Infinite connection doesn't promise you eternity, but it certainly delivers in intensity, wholeness and joy. True connection will eventually leave you enriched, better equipped and more healed than when you started.

I invite all my readers to pause and reflect on how you could (with awareness, ownership and responsibility) bring in any relationship a version of yourself that is empowered to shape the relationship from whatever it would be into a space of growth, progress and fulfilment.

Being 'connected' with your partner is more than a temporary feeling of happiness, it is a stable mental wellbeing that empowers you to live with 'joie de vivre' when times are good and to use your effective coping skills when times are challenging.

Even if you are twenty, fifty or seventy you can start at any point to create the relationship you want. Once you've reclaimed your wholeness and you have a clear vision about your partner and the relationship you want, you become unstoppable.

Chapter I

Dating... yourself

1.1. A glimpse into dating trends

Modern dating landscape looks very different than the traditional one. Prior to early 1900 the odds of choosing a partner were almost zero. Nevertheless, nowadays we have plenty of freedom to choose who we want to share our life with. The progress of technology made it possible to connect with people, regardless their location and it has offered us so many opportunities for finding love as never before.

The society has undergone an important shift regarding online dating, leaving the traditional face-to-face dating behind. While for most of us the goal has remained the same, to find true love and connection, how we date and find the people we date has radically changed.

Online dating promises numerous benefits from speed, convenience, flexibility to more potential matches and quick icebreakers. From the comfort of your home, from the metro or from work, the digital communication accelerates the interaction with a possible partner through instant messages or video calls. While this may feel really convenient, especially in the fast-paced environment we are living, we may miss out the genuine interaction and connection.

In the online dating the initial stages of a relationship upfold through virtual communication, therefore, we may skip various stages of our relationship. Online dating is portrayed as a form of fun, happy and exciting experience, but it can be misleading and have a serious impact on our mental health.

Unfortunately, not all the connections formed online support the reality. Also, a new way of therapy may be needed for those who experience challenges under the online dating process. While the whole connection created may be an illusion the emotions and feelings people experience through online dating are real and valid.

It is important to acknowledge the opportunities online dating provides us, but, at the same time, to understand its limitations.

Nothing can replace the face-to-face interactions and in-person chemistry connection.

Rather than focusing on the differences, the key is to incorporate elements from both face-to-face and online dating and to embrace the myriad ways in which we can find love.

The future of dating could evolve from cyber flirting to virtual romance filled with AI successors assisting the dating process. Nevertheless, our goal remains finding true love and genuine connection.

Key takeaways

Dating landscape has shifted from meeting someone face-to-face to online dating. Modern dating dynamics has its own pros and cons, and it impacts each and every one of us in different ways. While in future dating is expected to gain complexity, our ultimate goal remains finding true love and connection.

1.2. It all starts with you

The latest statistics* show that we are almost 8.2 billion people on Earth. As technology has reshaped the world and made the connection between people much easier than ever before, paradoxically it seems harder than ever to find a lifelong relationship.

Dating culture is constantly changing and it has encountered new stressors that previous generations didn't have to experience: managing social media, the culture of comparison, lack of time, just to name a few.

The current influencers and online trends promote the ideal partner/relationship

* According to Worldometer
https://www.worldometers.info/world-population/

filled with unrealistic standards and expectations that we must pursue. Chasing unreasonable standards has left many people looking for a partner feeling exhausted, disappointed and not good enough. It is a fact that dating can affect one's mental health in a way that varies from person to person.

Considering all these factors, it's no wonder that so many people are struggling with finding a partner. But something has to change. From rethinking cultural norms about the perfect partner/relationship to shifting perspectives from focusing on ourselves rather than the potential partner.

At the end of the day if you haven't done the work with yourself (one person) how can you commit to balance the differences between two people? If you don't know yourself, how can you authentically and intentionally bring your best self to a relationship? And how can you genuinely know the other?

In this chapter I will address a few aspects I believe we all need to explore before starting a relationship.

Firstly, before starting a relationship you need to go on a self-discovery journey in order to see who you are. You need to know yourself first, before anyone else. Only in this way you can start a relationship based on authenticity and consciousness.

When you focus on how you expect the other person to be, you tend to lose sight about the most important part you bring to a relationship which is yourself. Because it all starts with you...

Having a deep knowledge and understanding of yourself is the first step you need to consider before starting a relationship.

If you don't know your values, if your life principles are unclear or incongruent it's going to be really difficult to find another person or even when finding someone the relationship will be very fragile without a strong foundation.

Understanding who you are is empowering. It enables you to discover yourself and use all that information to become something more or different. By knowing who you are you can display in front of the other your true, authentic self and see if you make a good match.

Many people are looking for tips about how they should prepare for a first date but, truth be told, you just need to be yourself. You are not trying to impress someone who will never see you again. Creating a false impression about yourself will just, useless, complicate your future in dating. Instead, by showing your true self you can create a real, meaningful future connection no matter the way things turn out.

Secondly, you need to pay attention to your childhood. You may find different issues, traumas and/or other fixed patterns that need to be addressed if you want to have a conscious relationship. It's your duty to know your triggers, wounds, needs and childhood traumas and heal or manage them in order to avoid their negative impact on your relationship. Although there will be some wounds that will only show up when you are in a relationship, there are definitely some childhood issues that you can take accountability for, even when you are on your own.

The third aspect you need to consider is your inner dialogue. When you are thinking negative thoughts about yourself and feed your inner critic, it will influence the way you feel about yourself. Negative thoughts are unhelpful and unproductive. On the other hand, when you start talking to yourself in a positive way and you are kind to yourself, you increase your level of self-acceptance and understanding. Hence you can access the most beautiful and the most amazing version of yourself. And guess how you will show up in your relationship? Exactly how you feel about yourself.

The last aspect to consider is what you normalize. You need to pay close attention to your boundaries, to what you settle for and to what you normalize. Even if you are or not conscious about it, the only consistent 'thing' in all your relationships is yourself and you will recreate your old patterns in all your new relationships. That's why it all starts with you.

Key takeaways

Dating culture is constantly changing. There are four aspects I encourage you to explore before starting a relationship: self-discovery, your childhood, your inner dialogue and what you normalize. It is your job to go on a self-discovery journey in order to be authentic, empowered and conscious about how you will show up in your relationship. One of the most important things you can do for yourself is to understand who you are. You can tap into your inner beauty and access the most beautiful and the most amazing version of yourself.

Instead of expecting to find a good partner why not making the effort to becoming one first?

1.3. How are we self-sabotaging?

We all want to be happy, fall in love and live happily ever after. But, most of the times, this is not just happening to us, we need to create it. We have seen in the previous chapter that it is essential to know ourselves. In this chapter we will explore more about how we are self-sabotaging. Although it may sound counterintuitive, we are the ones who are sabotaging ourselves and our relationship most of the times. How, may you ask?

Well, sometimes conscious, sometimes unconscious.

Although at the surface you may spot some unhelpful behaviours like withdrawal, defensiveness, perfectionism, just to mention a few, the truth is that you need to pay attention to the root causes of these behaviours if you really want to improve. While self-sabotage can embrace very different forms of expression, I will analyse three of its most common root causes which are lack of experience, childhood wounds and low emotional intelligence. But, if I was to further narrow down, the major cause is lack of self-awareness. And I believe you intuitively guessed the cure: cultivating self-awareness.

Let's go back though to the lack of experience. Many times, in a relationship, the lack of experience will show up. As you evolve in your relationship you may encounter challenges that you haven't previously experienced, therefore you don't really know how to handle them. Well, while there may be many different approaches that lead to solutions, definitely tapping into your self-awareness is one of the best.

The lack of experience within a relationship can take different forms of self-sabotage from holding unrealistic views and expectations to acting in ways that are not serving you or the relationship. When what you expect doesn't match the reality, you can become frustrated and unhappy.

The views you hold about yourself, your partner and your relationship need to be based on reality. Shall they be based on illusions about reality without being backed up by facts, you will end up deceiving yourself and finding yourself in situations that lack optimal solutions. When you create issues from your unawareness, it's hard to solve them using rational approaches. Therefore, you may end up feeling trapped in the impossibility of finding optimal solutions which leads to self-sabotage.

Now it's time to move on to our second root cause of self-sabotage, the childhood wounds. We know very well by now that the connections with our first caregivers profoundly affect our adult relationships. Although, many times you may notice low self-esteem, insecure attachment style, unhealthy relationship beliefs, different fears like fear of getting hurt or fear of commitment etc. these are just effects of a deeper root cause: your childhood wounds. Unless you address them and heal as much as possible (remember, healing is a journey, not a destination) you are likely to recreate unhealthy patterns that will sabotage your relationship.

For instance, if you feel you are not (good) enough most probably you will reflect upon your partner all your insecurities through jealousy, lack of setting and communicating firm boundaries (but going to be upset when

29

they cross them), projecting different fears and expecting all your needs to be met. But if your partner does the same, the relationship can't function. You need to start your healing journey with compassion, responsibility and ownership, but mostly with self-awareness.

The third way that leads to self-sabotage is having low emotional intelligence. This means you allow your emotions to hijack you, you become easily triggered and you have little or no control over your emotions and reactions. When you have low emotional intelligence, you may display behaviours such as withdrawal, disrespect, emotional unavailability, poor emotional regulation etc. These are just the effects of low emotional intelligence.

It is your duty to become emotionally literate and learn how to recognize, understand and manage your emotions in ways that are serving you. Emotional triggers are frequent in relationships and, truth be told, many times you can only learn from your own experiences. Be patient, stay with your emotions and learn how to gain control over them.

Overall, self-awareness is the best antidote to self-sabotage. It is in the moment when you wake up and take charge, accountability and responsibility for your life that things change (you create the magic) and you learn to establish meaningful relationships.

Key takeaways

We are sabotaging ourselves and our relationships whether we realize it or not. In any case, the results are going to be the same: dysfunctional relationships, frustration, unhappiness and breaking up. Although there are many ways in which self-sabotage is displayed in our relationships from defensiveness, perfectionism, withdrawal etc., here I've drawn attention towards a few of its root causes including lack of experience, childhood wounds and low emotional intelligence. You need to correct and address the root causes to see different outcomes.

The best antidote for self-sabotage is self-awareness. You have within you the power and resources to create the relationship you want.

Chapter II
Falling in love

2.1. Finding the ideal partner

We live in a world full of perfect people. If you scroll on social media, you can, with just a click, find the most beautiful, rich and well-travelled people. However, when you look around, you may ask yourself: where are all these people?

Or sometimes you may meet someone 'perfect' and notice that the reality is slightly different. While the online has helped us a lot in finding partners especially during the latest years nevertheless it has also contributed to many deceiving and disappointing experiences.

In this chapter I will walk you through three steps that will better prepare yourself to find the ideal partner. Supposing you did the work with yourself (remember, it's a process), now it's time to focus on the next steps.

The first one is to know what you want, to know who your ideal partner is. One of the reasons why many people end up in wrong relationships is that they have no idea what they want. Therefore, they end up accepting whoever they meet thinking that it may work or that people may change. Ideally, you would know what you want regarding your partner, but the bare minimum you can do, is, at least, to know who you don't want. If it's hard for you to have a clear image of the person you'd like to meet you can instead find a few features, values, personality traits you really don't want and flip them over. In this way you will have a clear vision about the person you'd like to start a relationship with.

Another step is to stop looking for the perfect partner. Expecting to find a perfect partner it's an illusion that you could give up right now. Do you know the story with the man who was looking for the perfect partner, but he remained single? He was really old, and a friend asked him: 'How it comes that from so many people that are living on the Earth you never found the perfect one?' 'I did find', said the old man. 'And why you're not together then?', his friend asked. 'Well, she was also looking for the perfect man'. The truth is perfection is an unrealistic standard and nobody is perfect, not even you. A better approach would be to replace perfection with compatibility. Finding someone who makes a good match, who is compatible with you, it's a nice expectation to hold. Although it may take time and effort it's really worth it. Nothing is more precious than having a partner who is in alignment with you and who makes the relationship grow harmoniously. In any case, you don't need to lose sight of the third step: be ready to compromise.

The third step is to be ready to compromise. You must be aware that you can't find everything in one person therefore you will need to compromise.

Be ready to meet the other person where they are and learn to accommodate the differences. This doesn't mean lowering your standards or settling for less than what you want, but, understanding that no two people are alike and it's normal to work on the existing differences. However, even if working on a relationship may feel hard sometimes, it shouldn't be painful. While you need to give enough time to meet, understand and know the other, be ready to accept that you may find someone who may not have the ability or willingness to love you as you want. Don't waste your time and energy by trying and trying to 'fix' a partner who seems wrong from the beginning. Instead pay attention and believe people when they show you who they are. If your gut feeling senses something wrong, you may want to trust it. A relationship needs to make you feel good, not to be a constant struggle.

Key takeaways

Expecting to find a perfect partner is an unrealistic standard. Focus instead on knowing what you want, on finding a compatible person and on being ready to compromise. A relationship is not meant to be perfect, but real.

2.2. Do you know who you are with?

On a long-term, meaningful relationship, it is essential to get to know your partner in order to create the relationship you want. Curiosity is the secret ingredient that can truly make the difference. And here I'm not referring only to know about your partner's favourite food, or movie, but also about boundaries, attachment style, love language, vulnerabilities and so on. When you are actively involved in a relationship you get precious clues, verbal and nonverbal, about your partner. Then, it is up to you to use them for fostering the initial connection.

Since in the early stages of a relationship partners are more likely to idealize each other, it is really important to grow in knowledge regarding your potential partner. The sooner you do this, the more time and resources you save by eliminating a partner that is not suitable for you. Knowing your potential partner should ideally be a never-ending process of discovering and understanding of your partner's personality, core values, past experiences, vulnerabilities and expectations.

Even if we are intentional about it, this process doesn't occur instantly, it will take time. As much as we may want to know our partner's reality, we will only get to know them to the degree the other person allows themselves to be known. Therefore, we increase the probability of an authentic relationship and connection with another individual by getting more access into their world. But how can you enter their world?

Well, the best way to connect with your partner is to create, within the relationship, a space where the other person feels safe and secure to share with you everything, including their vulnerabilities. When your partner feels threatened, it is likely that they show you little from their 'hidden world'. And this may sometimes be done unconsciously, as human beings will do anything to avoid rejection. Therefore, being open, curious and non-judgmental can prove to be your strong allies in the journey of discovering your partner.

Most of the times, when we fall in love, we focus on learning our partner's preferences, likes and dislikes, however this surface level understanding may not be all we truly need to know. In order to be able to establish a deep connection, there are a few more things that we really need to know about our partner like their personality, their values, their beliefs, their expectations, their emotional heritage and so on. Let's take a glance at these aspects:

Personality - although personality can't predict compatibility between partners, it will definitely play a crucial role in your relationship. For instance, you don't need to be a psychologist to understand if the person you are dating with is introvert or extrovert, pessimistic or optimistic, more adventurous or safer etc.

Values - the values a person holds create their identity. It is important to know somebody's values from the very beginning. Rarely can people with contrasting values make it work, but, luckily, we will distance from people with different values, even unconsciously.

41

Beliefs - each of us possess a set of beliefs that shapes our views about the world and ourselves. While as partners, we may and will not agree on everything, it is important to see how the world of your potential partner looks like. Maybe women are from Venus and men are from Mars[1], but before you find the common ground, you may need to visit the partner's world and understand how things are there. This reminds me of a joke: 'When John and Mary got married, he asked: "What shall we do now? We live my life or yours?"'.

Expectations - as we've seen that nobody is here to please our expectations. You need to be able to distinguish between reasonable expectations and unrealistic expectations, or in other words demands. The

---

1   Referring to John Gray, *Men Are from Mars, Women Are from Venus: a Practical Guide for Improving Communication and Getting What You Want in Your Relationships, New York: Harper Collins, 1992.*

first step in setting expectations is learning how to communicate them clearly, openly and efficiently with our partner. Stop expecting the other person can read your mind, all you'll do is to get frustrated. Instead, shouldn't be better to explicit communicate your partner what you really expect from them?

Emotional heritage - the family of origin, the first caregivers, as well as previous relationships, leave us useful tracks of understanding our partners' current needs and behaviours. Often, you may get precious information about your partner's emotional reactivity, vulnerabilities, needs, wants and blueprints about how they think relationship works if you look at the family of origin (his/her family), their interactions and in his/her childhood.

So on – I obviously can't mention everything here, but you've got my point. Look deeper at the other and notice their mindset, habits, needs, health, rituals etc. Once you start a relationship with someone, all of these will influence you too.

Key takeaways

Dive into the other's world with willingness and curiosity to get to know your partner rather than with judgment and/or criticism. You can only access 'that much' of a person's world and that's OK. The more open and authentic you are, the more likely it is that the other person reveals their true self.

There is more to know about the other than what their favourite movie or food is. When choosing a partner, it is your duty and responsibility to dig beyond the surface and focus on aspects like personality, values, beliefs, expectations and emotional heritage and so on. When you understand there are two realities, two different worlds, equally important, to harmonize, you can shift your focus on the relationship itself. And, in that moment, you open the possibility to create a new, combined, better life and relationship.

2.3. Falling in love versus being in love

Many of us to confuse the process of falling in love with being in love. I know we haven't learned it in school, but only if you become able to distinguish between these two processes, you are likely to have a conscious and fulfilling relationship. Let's take them one by one for a better understanding.

Falling in love is a chemical process, a release of neurotransmitters in the brain that makes us feel good. The characteristics required to fall in love with someone can be peculiar, superficial and changeable: physical attractiveness, proximity, perceived compatibility just to name a few. For instance, you can fall in love when you meet someone who feels familiar, when someone has the ability to meet your unmet needs or for any other reason: chemistry, other similarities etc.

The relationship can work perfectly in the beginning, however, if there is not compatibility based on rational thinking and common values, it is meant to fail. Falling in love is based on physical attraction, which comes from our primary instincts. Even so, this is not enough to be lifetime with that person. Sooner or later the passion will be gone, and, in that moment, you are left with values, vision, rational thinking etc. If you don't align these with your partner, it is absolutely normal to have a dysfunctional relationship filled with frustration, disappointment and conflict. Most of the times we fall in love with the projection of the ideal partner reflected on the person in front of us. However, when this person doesn't become who we expected we may feel we've lost the connection. The truth is that when we fall in love with the potentiality of what we imagined that person could be, once the person reveals themselves as they are, we may feel disappointment and sadness.

On the other hand, being in love is a conscious choice we make based on rational criteria. Being in love requires patience and commitment rather than just expecting things to be good. It requires responsibility and willingness to respect the other's boundaries, meet your partner where they are and love your partner the way they need you to show

47

up. Being in love goes far beyond the physical attraction between two people, and it's about dating your partner's visions, values and rational thinking rather than just instincts.

When we confuse falling in love with being in love, we end up deceiving ourselves. Why? Because we are 'Homo sapiens' and besides our primary needs, a relationship is about much more. Being in love is the complex state that that transforms an ordinary relationship into an extraordinary one.

Key takeaways

Many people confuse falling in love with being in love. Falling in love is a chemical process based on the attraction you feel in the initial stage of a relationship. Being in love is a conscious choice that requires a different level of bonding and connecting with a partner. You need to be able to distinguish between falling in love and being in love while cherishing and fully enjoying your relationship journey.

Chapter III
Your relationship

3.1. Is your relationship healthy?

Why is so hard to create meaningful and healthy relationships if, supposing, both partners want this? While there are many possible answers to this question, the most common response is that we may not know exactly how to create healthy relationships.

Unfortunately, the skills we need to start and sustain a healthy relationship are not taught to us formally, but rather modelled to us by our family members. Therefore, guided by our inner compass, we develop several ideas about how a healthy relationship should look like.

Although healthy relationships may be defined in different ways, there are some key elements that you could consider when you assess the health of your relationship:

- There is a safe space where you feel free (comfortable) to communicate your thoughts, feelings and vulnerabilities.

- Your relationship is based on love, honesty, respect and mutual trust.

- The presence of effective conflict management and ability to resolve differences of opinion.

- You have an increased self-awareness of behaviours and actions.

- You set and respect boundaries.

- You make each other a priority.

- You celebrate each other's success and growth.

- Both partners take ownership, accountability and responsibility.

- You feel at ease in your relationship.

- You look forward to spending time with each other.

This is by no means an exhaustive list, but it is meant to offer you an overall guidance to refresh your awareness of what a healthy relationship contains. What you need to remember is that healthy relationships don't just happen to us, instead they take time and intention to be built and co-created. They require from both partners several abilities such as willingness, patience, communication, respect, adjustments, recognizing problems, navigating through conflict, even identifying possible threats to the long-term health of your relationship etc.

Even if your relationship seems healthy, it can, at any time deteriorate, if left unattended. Be willing to analyse your relationship and look for any improvements you can make for a healthier and fulfilling relationship.

Key takeaways

Building a healthy relationship it's not easy, but it is achievable, and it should be desirable too.

Your relationship is your choice. You deserve to be in a healthy, happy and loving relationship. There are certain key elements that a healthy relationship contains. It's important to remember that with self-awareness you have the power to create the relationship you want.

3.2. All you need is love

Is love really all we need? Maybe it used to be like this once, when our only concern regarding a relationship was our primary needs: survival and reproduction. Today the concept of love has gained complexity, and we are looking for much more from our partner and from our relationship.

We have changed, we have become more mindful, more selfish some may say, but it is clear we pay more attention to the way in which love is expressed. We want love on our terms, and we are not willing to settle for less than we think we deserve.

Truth be told your relationship will be as good as your inner hidden self-image. When you lack self-confidence, when you are insecure, you will reflect these lacks in your relationship by being clingy, requiring constant attention and validation etc. You can only create an abundant relationship if you are abundant. As they say, 'you can't pour from an empty cup'.

While love on our terms may vary from person to person, from one love language to another, I think we can all agree on some aspects. When we think about a potential partner, we think about intentionality, commitment, responsibility, intimacy, ownership, someone to honour and respect us and so on. We don't want just 'a nice person' to hang with, but somebody who is ready to walk the talk. We don't view love as a form of idealization anymore, instead, we need clear, tangible actions consistent with the promises we've been given.

We have realized that the relationship is a space of fulfilment and that we can't evolve if we are in a relationship where we are constantly pulled back. We hold standards for ourselves, our partner and our relationship and it's OK. Beware to craft the appropriate standards in the light of the specific relationship. Make sure that you, your partner and your relationship support the standards you require.

Ultimately, the biggest thing to keep in mind is that you and only you define what is acceptable for yourself. Just because something is normalized, it doesn't mean that you need to integrate it in your relationship.

Therefore 'all you need is love' is a statement that is incomplete. While love is indeed a necessary ingredient for happiness, a relationship is about much more.

Key takeaways

The way in which love is manifested is going to determine our happiness and fulfilment. Your relationship will be all as good as your inner hidden self-image. When you paint the red flags, green, and lower your standards you will end up in the wrong story. Remember, you need more than love to make a relationship work.

3.3. The miracle of now

One of the hardest things to do in a relationship is not to do something: just to be present. In an era full of distractions, we often may take for granted what is the most valuable: the miracle of now.

Learning to live in the 'now', can prove to be beneficial not only for you, but for your partner and your relationship too.

Many times, we tend to worry about the past or to project ourselves in the future, while forgetting to enjoy the now, the present moment. In reality, all you have is now and the more you learn to focus on the present moment, the more conscious, mindful and happy you can be. Before being present in a relationship, it is important to develop a connection with one's self.

You need to train yourself to appreciate the daily interactions, the most ordinary moments and to allow the relationship to unfold naturally, without trying to plan your next move. Staying present in the moment allows you to enjoy every step and stage of your relationship, without any requirements from your partner.

However, because you've been taught that you always need to do something you may find it challenging to just be present, free of any activity or control. One of the most common mistakes people make in relationships is to wait for certain, 'perfect' moments to foster connection. You have every day the opportunity to connect with your partner, at any given time.

When you learn to be present and live every moment at its full intensity, with spontaneity, you get the power to enjoy your relationship free of doubt, worry, regrets, or fear. You accept the relationship as it is and you don't look for the perfect one. Only when you start cherishing your relationship for what it is rather than what it should be, you step into a magic land of reality, presence and consciousness.

We tend to assess our relationship based on previous, past filters about how it should be until we realise that what's happening it's exactly what it should happen and at the right timing.

When we become aware about this, we can embrace spontaneity, give up fixed patterns from our past and enjoy the present moment as it is. And what can be more beautiful than to be in the 'here and now'?

Sometimes we underestimate the power of the moment, but it is in the small moments that we get the most joy: a hug, a kiss, a look in the eyes...these make the difference between connected and complacent relationships.

Key takeaways

Starting to live in the 'here and now' can be a real gamechanger for your relationship. When you are anchored in the present moment you get the opportunity to enjoy every single moment and elevate your relationship.

Chapter IV
When the ships sink

4.1. The four horsemen

If you are intentional about making your relationship better, you might have heard about the Gottman Institute. Drs. John and Julie Gottman have dedicated their life to study love, healthy relationships and, as well, failing relationships. In this chapter, the focus will be on the research regarding the four horsemen that can spoil any relationship and their antidotes.

The four Horsemen are four dysfunctional patterns of navigating conflict that can predict the upcoming failure of a relationship. Although conflicts are inevitable part of our relationships, the way in which we handle conflict can prove to be either beneficial or the detrimental to our relationship, leading us towards happiness or failure.

According to Dr. Gottman there are four slow killers or 'the four Horsemen' in a relationship: criticism, contempt, defensiveness and stonewalling. Let's take them one by one for a better understanding.

Criticism represents a verbal attack at the core of someone's character or personality. Rather than addressing the actual issue, it attacks the person. Some examples of criticisms could be "you are lazy" or "you always... ". With such an approach, the discussion can escalate into an argument. Instead, criticism could be replaced by a gentle startup, a more productive way of expressing your feelings using "I" or "I feel..." statements.

In this way, you avoid blaming the other and you focus on solving the issue by expressing your feelings about it. For example, instead of "you are lazy", you can say "I feel frustrated/angry/upset...because I get to do all the work", or "could you help me with/ I need you to... (specific task)". When your partner doesn't feel attacked, it's more likely to respond positively to your need.

The second one, content, represents an attempt of insulting or making your partner feel worthless by using a position of moral superiority. Some examples of contempt include eye, rolling, mocking, sarcasm, etc.

Whoever had a longer relationship must be familiar with them by now. Joke aside, contempt has proved to be the strongest predictor of divorce or separation. It leaves the partner disrespected and it can easily create resentments.

The antidote to contempt is appreciation. Appreciation offers you the opportunity to cultivate respect, gratitude and affection in other words to love and honour your partner. Dr. Gottman speaks about the 5 to 1 "magic ratio" of positive to negative interactions which means that you need five positive interactions for every negative one.

The third horsemen, defensiveness, makes you find excuses and victimizing yourself in front of a perceived attack.

The antidote for defensiveness is to take responsibility without blaming your partner. When you empathize with your partner and validate your partners' feelings, you can effectively work towards a compromise.

The last one, stonewalling, is an avoidance of the conflict which happens when an individual feels overwhelmed. Therefore, the reaction is to shut down, stop responding and disengage.

The antidote in the situation would be to practice, psychological self-soothing. It means taking a break that should last for at least 20 minutes and doing something that is psychologically soothing. In this way, you can return to the initial conversation ready to approach the discussion more rational, productive and positive.

Key takeaways

It is up to you to learn strategies to improve the way you manage conflict in your relationship. There is research that comes with effective, proven alternatives to help you create a stable and happy relationship. Conflicts won't solve miraculously, or just fade away, instead they need to be addressed and handled in healthy ways.

4.2. Betrayal

When we think about relationships, infidelity is one of the scariest words that comes to our mind. But, in reality, there are deeper underlying issues to be addressed. It's not the infidelity, but the betrayal that holds the responsibility of the violation of trust.

We all know that mutual trust lays the foundation of any relationship. It is a basic and irreplaceable requirement for a relationship to function and thrive. You can foster trust in your relationship during daily interactions.

Trust is an implicit agreement between you and your partner that strengthens the bond in any relationship. On the other hand, in dysfunctional relationships, you can find pieces and pieces of broken trust on the floor: disloyalty, conditional commitment, dishonesty, and so on. When the trust is broken, excuses become irrelevant.

Sometimes betrayal may be loud and obvious like an affair for instance, while other times betrayal may be subtle and silent, and it may sneak into your life without even noticing it. In that case betrayal is an accumulation of altered behaviours that proceeded the sink of the ship: an 'innocent' flirt, a shared vulnerability with a colleague, a lack of support towards partner, and so on.

I know relationships may seem complicated, but, when you take time and reflect upon the context of your particular relationship certain facts will make sense. It may be hard to accept it or take responsibility or ownership, but it will make sense.

Things rarely happen in vain, instead they are cultivated on a vulnerable ground of avoidance, rejection and negativity.

The effects of betrayal in your life are complex and can have a long-lasting impact on your mental health. Betrayal trauma may include self-doubt, mistrust, rumination, hyper vigilance, anxiety, anger, guilt, shame and may leave deep traces that will need to be addressed and healed.

One can never fully protect against betrayal. Instead, you can understand that people are going to act according to their level of understanding at a certain point and this has nothing to do with you.

Key takeaways

Betrayal can be as loud as an affair or as silent as a chain of actions that compromise the implicit mutual trust and alters the bond between two partners. Most of the times, infidelity is a consequence of betrayal, not its cause.

The traces that betrayal leave will impact your mental health and shouldn't be left unchecked. Healing is possible and necessary for your better future.

4.3. How to recognise a toxic relationship

Relationships are part of our life, but not all of them are healthy. Although we have seen earlier the characteristics of healthy relationships, in this chapter toxic relationships will be carefully analysed. Even if it started good, any relationship could spiral into a toxic one, at any point.

It is your responsibility to educate yourself about the signs and about the consequences a toxic relationship can bring to your life and to find the courage to leave such a relationship immediately.

Toxic relationships are more than occasional moments of tension. Unfortunately, they are harmful dynamics of consistently manipulating and undermining yourself and your values.

Although there are examples of toxic relationships all around us, when they are happening to us, we may dismiss the signs that likewise are so obvious. On the other hand, if you grew up in a house where yelling or devaluing yourself was a part of your daily life, this may be your normal standard. But not anymore!

Identifying toxic relationships isn't always straightforward. Toxic relationships can sometimes be hard to spot since they may look like loving ones, but they are not. "What is the difference?", you may ask. Well, they make you feel drained, stressed, overwhelmed or afraid all the time.

Sometimes the shift from a healthy to a toxic relationship can happen so gradually that you can hardly even notice.

Having the ability to recognize red flags early can save you a lot of trouble. Although hard to swallow, red flags are clear indicators of any toxic relationship. Let's see some examples of red flags:

- Physical, sexual or emotional abuse.

- Dishonesty.

- The relationship is too demanding.

- Frequent orders, demands, ultimatums and requests.

- Loss of integrity.

- Unpredictability.

- Controlling behaviours, manipulative tactics.

- Ignoring your needs.

- Social media harassment, or threats.

- Masking control as care.

- You are consistently disrespected.

- You are feeling always stressed around your partner.

- You have compromised all your boundaries.

- You are being devalued or disregarded.

These are some of the most common red flags that you shouldn't ignore. Also, digital dimensions of toxic relationships are not to be overlooked. If you notice these red flags in your relationship, you need to take action. "Yes, but what can I do?", you may ask.

If we are talking about abuse, you need to end the relationship immediately. The abuse of any form it's not getting any better.

If the relationship is not abusive, you can decide whether to work on improving it or moving on. No one can tell you how or when it's time to end your relationship. Keep in mind though that repairing it's possible only if both parties are willing to make the necessary changes.

The paradox of toxic relationships is that many of us stay in a toxic relationship long beyond its expiration date. Be it from denial, hope, fear or any other reason, we may procrastinate and stay for a little too long before leaving a toxic relationship. Even so, the more we postpone that moment, the harder it becomes to find our way out of it. When you are in denial, you may find excuses for your partner's behaviour. The only message you are sending is that you are OK tolerating this.

Another reason why it seems so hard to end a toxic relationship it's the hope. There is always the "what if" question in our mind: "what if s/he changes?", "what if s/he is the one?". Your idealization of the reality will neither fix the relationship, nor change how things actually are. And as much as you wish to help the other, no one can change unless they want it or they are ready for it.

Regarding the fear, it's never easy to end a toxic relationship. You need to be brave and remember that you always have a choice. The courage that will get you out from a toxic relationship may be the same courage that will lead you to find a healthier relationship. Challenging times are often disguised opportunities for growing.

No one deserves to be in a toxic relationship. It is not normal, not acceptable and definitely not your fault.

Your emotional well-being should be your priority and, whenever threatened, you must immediately address and resolve the issue that put it at risk. You also need to be aware that ending a relationship won't necessarily sort out all your problems overnight.

Remember, a relationship is not something happening to you, but something that you choose daily. Finding your way out from a toxic relationship may be your ticket for happiness and wellbeing.

Key takeaways

Toxic relationships are more frequent than we would like to admit. Relationships are never perfect, and we may encounter misunderstandings and differences that will need to be balanced. However, when you find many red flags in your relationship, it may be time to leave.

Ending a relationship is never easy, but sometimes it's necessary. Staying a bit too long and illuding yourself that things will improve won't change the reality. Your well-being should be your priority. You have the right to be happy and choose someone who chooses you every single day.

Chapter V
A Straight A relationship

5.1. Acceptance

Acceptance is the first A grade any relationship receives. Along with Authenticity and Autonomy, they represent key elements for a straight A relationship. As human beings, we are wired for connection to feel fully alive. And, at the very foundation of connection, lays acceptance.

In relationships, acceptance can be regarded from two perspectives the acceptance of one's partner and one own's feeling of being accepted. But what is acceptance? Acceptance is seeing the reality as it is. Accepting your partner is seeing who your partner is at this very moment in time.

If you're struggling with your partner's acceptance, I invite you to take a look at yourself. In order to unconditionally accept somebody, you need to accept yourself first. Self-acceptance means unconditionally accepting yourself as you are and, if you want to take a step further, knowing that you are enough.

When you don't hold this perception about yourself, you will neither feel accepted, nor be able to accept your partner. You may fall into the trap to gain acceptance and validation from your relationship, and you will, eventually, find yourself settling for breadcrumbs.

Working hard to prove your value and feel accepted is a sign of lack of self-acceptance that will only lead to co-dependency and unhealthy relationships.

Relationship acceptance doesn't mean that you need to agree or tolerate bad habits or behaviours. The reality is as it is, even if you give your consent or not. When you don't like a behaviour, you can choose how you wish to respond. Besides, if you want to create any change in your relationship, the best you can do is to plant the seeds of love and acceptance instead of criticism and judgement. In any case, acceptance is something that needs to be experienced rather than conceptualized.

There are countless benefits that acceptance brings you in a relationship: balance, harmony, safety, liberation, freedom

83

and much more. Also, it can help you reduce anxiety or disappointments by being more attuned to reality. You need to meet people where they are, and you need to be able to let go of unrealistic and unnecessary expectations.

Acceptance requires awareness, presence and essence. In relationships there are always going to be challenges and differences to reconcile and it's up to us to put barriers or to build bridges towards authentic connections.

Key takeaways

You deserve a relationship where both you and your partner are accepted for who you are. Yet, you will only accept your partner if you have accepted yourself first. Acceptance has the power to reconcile differences and help you let go of your expectancies in order to create space for a person to be who they are.

Last, but not least, love starts with acceptance, and it is an essential prerequisite for a thriving relationship.

5.2. Relationship Authenticity

Society and social media may often put a tremendous amount of pressure to showcase the idealized version of ourselves and our relationship. Unfortunately, nowadays, relationships' authenticity has become something more wished than experienced.

On riding the carousel of perfection, we may lose sight of authenticity, which along with love represents the essence of life. Establishing an authentic relationship is a

85

process that may require time and intention. There is no time frame in discovering your authenticity, but if you intentionally choose this road you'll get there. Keep in mind there are no shortcuts though.

The only way in which you can create an authentic relationship in your life is to discover your authenticity. We have seen from the very first chapter that all starts with you, with self-discovery and self-love. Being authentic and living in harmony with your true essence is one of the most important assets you may have.

Authenticity allows you to genuinely connect with another person and to create a unique bond. This bond is developed by sharing your deepest thoughts, fears, emotions, hopes and dreams without fearing judgement or criticism.

Authentic partners are able to give and receive unconditional love. Your aim is to cultivate a relationship where you are seen and honoured for who you are instead of displaying a false image of yourself. When you are too concerned to play the role of the perfect partner, you may forget to be the right partner. And more than this, you may end up forgetting who you really are...

Authenticity also fosters intimacy allowing two individuals to connect at a more profound level. Definitely it requires vulnerability as you may be criticized, judged or even rejected. But if your relationship is not a safe space to express your vulnerabilities and flaws, is it even worth it? If your authenticity conflicts love, you should never compromise. Shall the relationship's cost be your authenticity, then it's too expensive.

In any case, authenticity is about yourself, it's about who you truly are. When you harmonize your inner with your outer essence, authenticity will empower you to take ownership and develop a truly meaningful relationship with another person who is willing and able to accept, love and honour you for who you are. Isn't that the greatest gift you can receive?

Key takeaways

Intentionally creating an authentic relationship is a goal worth pursuing. In such a relationship your authenticity is never threatened or conditioned but, on the contrary, you are loved and encouraged to be your true self. Trading your authenticity for love will result in a dysfunctional relationship leaving you drained and misunderstood.

Authentic relationships are the foundation of a meaningful and happy life. Authenticity fortifies the connection between two individuals by allowing them to be themselves around each other.

5.3. Romantic Autonomy

Many people buy into the idea that making a relationship your priority means giving up your personal autonomy. The purpose is to make the relationship a priority while maintaining your personal autonomy. It sounds good, but how is it even possible?

Well, being in a relationship and being autonomous are two compatible ideas. The challenging part here is to create a mutual support, connection and intimacy while retaining some independence. It may not be easy to create a balance, but it's possible.

The level of autonomy that each relationship supports may vary. Therefore, the people involved in a relationship will have to establish what works best for them. Too much autonomy may lead to separation, slowly finding yourself disconnected from your partner and on a totally different path. On the flipside, too much closeness can be smothering, and you may end up feeling trapped and lacking self-expression. Therefore, you and your partner will need to mutually agree upon a dynamic balance.

While sometimes you may need a closer connection and intimacy, other times, you may feel suffocated by it. So, in long term relationships, the balance is likely to change over time. It is really important to share your wants and needs for personal space with your partner and to listen to what the other person wants and needs too. In healthy relationships partners offer each other space to grow and expand. They don't feel threatened when they hear their partner may need some space, but quite the opposite, they offer, support and encourage autonomy.

The paradox of autonomy is that the more space you offer, the closer the partner is coming and on the contrary, the more you try to keep someone close, the more they feel they need to escape.

By encouraging autonomy, you are empowering your partner to show up with confidence and independence. On the other hand, controlling, manipulating, conditioning or owning the other are coming from your own fears, insecurities, and lack of self-worth and shall you cultivate these in our relationship they will reflect back on you.

91

A better perspective is to allow yourself and your partner to go back-and-forth until you are able to synchronize. Ultimately you will shape your future, and you will experience a relationship filled with growth and fulfilment.

Key takeaways

We should intentionally cocreate relationships that focus on growing and expanding rather than limiting our mutual autonomy. Relationships are like mirrors; they will reflect back to you whatever you give. Cultivating autonomy in your relationship offers you the opportunity to maintain a sense of self while being closely connected to your partner.

Autonomy is a vital aspect of a relationship's growth as it offers both partners a space to blossom with confidence and independence.

Chapter VI
Happily ever after

6.1. Contemplating hope

From the moment we meet someone we are full of hopes 'I hope this is the one!', 'I hope we will be together forever!', 'I hope my life will change.' etc. While hope can be comforting, it is not enough.

The future of your relationship shouldn't be regarded with fear and anxiety, but allowed with faith, hope and acceptance to unfold naturally, as it eventually will.

We have a need for certainty, and in order to satisfy this need our brain makes predictions. By combining elements from our past, with our understanding of current circumstances, we want to estimate how the future will look like. Sometimes the relationship can feel so good that we are concerned about preserving it as it is in the current moment.

Certain levels of hope can make you feel better and give you a good perspective about the future. That's fine but hope alone is not the solution. You need to allow hope to empower you and couple of it with actions.

It is important to understand that you never know what future may bring, and that there are no guarantees to make a relationship last forever. Not the priest, nor the mayor can promise a love to last forever, and nor you can do it. Any relationship can and will change in unpredictable ways, at unexpected times.

Sometimes you will experience your best life, while other times you'll have your dark moments. Also, nowadays, relationships have radically changed. We are navigating unknown territories, without a map, trying to find the right path through continuously adapting to changing circumstances.

The success of a relationship is not any more measured by its longevity as it used to be, but by its fulfilment, joy, growth, happiness, and so on. If these elements are missing, the relationship is over. We used to believe that longevity was a criterion for fulfilment, but not anymore.

Hope is a driving force, but you shouldn't count exclusively on it. More than this, instead of trying to predict the future, the best you can do is to live in the present moment. You are the one who designs your path guided by your intuition, hope and faith.

Let's contemplate hope with intention and action and allow it to empower us. Isn't it wonderful how much freedom we have today to create our relationships? We have the power to raise our standards to fulfilling relationships rather than just hope about them.

Key takeaways

Hope is a vital force that works best when it's coupled with action. Nowadays, relationships have been revolutionized and we are forced to find the map on the way. We have so much freedom, as never before, to create the relationships we want. In lack of any guarantees, let's elevate hope by taking actions for the better future of our relationship.

We are living miraculous times when we can choose to have a relationship based on love, fulfilment and progress. Isn't it amazing?

6.2. Inner state

A secret that nobody tells you about relationships is that your inner state dictates how fulfilling your relationship will be.

All our relationships are nothing but reflections of our inner world. That's why I want to go back to You and bring your awareness towards yourself. Of course, for a relationship to function we need 2 people, but you only have control over one of them which is YOU and, in consequence, upon your actions, your behaviours, your choices and so on.

Your relationship is going to be a projection of your inner state. So, if you don't like what you see on the outside, you have the possibility to change it by calibrating the inside.

Do you remember in the beginning of your relationship when you felt joy and excitement about the other person? It's because you were joyful and excited. If you take time to reflect on your relationship, you can notice how you create more and more of what you radiate.

Therefore, the only source of happiness or unhappiness in your relationship is you.

Sometimes, when you are unhappy in a relationship, you just got someone to put the blame on: 'Oh, I'm unhappy because my partner is not doing this...', but if you look better, it's all coming from inside and has nothing to do with your partner. It's your agenda about how s/he should do the things that is bothering you, not the other person.

In order to understand how powerful you are, you need to answer a simple question. What are your beliefs about the ideal relationship? The answer to this question is mainly a reflection of a long-held belief you have about relationships. This answer is going to be visible in the patterns you bring with you in your relationship.

If you think 'relationships are hard work', you will create your relationship to match this 'ideal'; instead, if you think 'relationships should be fulfilling', you will build meaningful relationships. Your thoughts, whether positive or not, will find a way to materialize in your life.

Your inner state is of major importance in all your relationships, but especially in your romantic relationship. When you feel good about yourself, when you are confident and worthy of love, you enter a relationship from a space of freedom and wholeness. And when you focus on the good parts, you will cultivate and experience more positive relationships.

On the other hand, when you feel bad about yourself, you will cultivate this in our relationship by focusing on criticism instead of appreciation, by turning your attention towards what is missing instead of what you have. And guess how your relationship it's going to look like?

Yes, but being at your best every day may seem a hard task... well, it's true, and it may not be a realistic goal. Being the best version of yourself doesn't mean you are always happy, that's toxic positivity. It means that you are the best you can be at a certain moment in time, and you are conscious about it. You can have a bad state, but you don't have to stay too much there unless you want to. Instead, if you want to have a happy relationship you can learn how to break your bad state. You can do this with awareness and gratitude.

It is a process of starting your day with the intention of showing up for yourself and for your partner. It is taking ownership of your relationship and understand that you are creating your relationship.

When you understand that the inner state is not brought by certain stimuli like your partner or autopilot, you realize that you can change it in a moment, not by magical thinking, but my conscious thinking. And in this moment, you're stepping in your full state of being and you are ready to overflow.

Key takeaways

Your inner state dictates how fulfilling your relationship will be. The beliefs you hold about relationships are going to be reflected in your relationship by revealing patterns that you carry in all your relationships, consciously or not.

You need to reflect and break the patterns that are not serving you. Remember, you have the power to create your inner state, and you'd better use it.

6.3. Growing new together

The relationship you create can become your most inspiring dream or your scariest nightmare. Your partner can be your biggest fan or your most dangerous enemy.

Taking enough time to find the right partner can prove to be the best life decision you've ever taken. Nothing compares to a fulfilling relationship where you feel seen, heard, valued and honoured.

Therefore, you we shouldn't pursue the perfect relationship, which is an illusion. Instead, you could focus on designing a true and authentic relationship.

To have a fulfilling relationship is not a fantasy and it doesn't require you to work so hard for it. Actually, it is more hard work in unhealthy relationships: constant conflict, chronic stress and powerless struggles that leave your stuck, drained, and unfulfilled. On the other hand, I'd say the Pareto principle, known as 80/20 rule, also applies in the healthy and fulfilling relationships: 20% of the input will generate 80% of your outcomes.

A healthy and fulfilling relationship is a transformative journey of change and growth that includes new insights, consciousness, acceptance and the willingness and availability to become a new version of yourself.

While changes are inevitable in any relationship, growth it's optional. The way you think about, feel about and engage in your relationship is going to transform your life.

Establishing a deep connection with your partner requires among others, building a solid foundation, having the right mindset, setting a few daily routines, handling conflict and adapting to unexpected changes.

As we have seen, building a relationship on acceptance, autonomy and authenticity support partners through their journey towards self-discovery and well-being. It creates a safe space and an anchor for whenever you feel confused or challenged.

It is up to you to adopt the mindset to embrace challenges with compassion, humour and wisdom. Eventually, our attitude will shape our relationship.

The right mindset allows you to embrace change and envision positive outcomes. Training yourself to look for the good things will generate a better perspective, more positive experiences and a happy life.

The difference between fulfilling and unfulfilling relationships lays in the habits, the daily routines the partners create (consciously or not). It's your choice to establish the hallmark of your relationship: what's your normality, what standards you live up to, what patterns you cultivate in your relationship and how your daily interactions look like.

Setting some daily routines of checking in with your partner, showing curiosity and appreciation are 'details' that can and will impact your relationship more than you think, both in good times and in times of struggle.

Best relationships don't fear or avoid conflict, instead, their partners learn how to handle it. Healthy conflict can be a great opportunity for couples to understand that they are in the same team.

Developing your ability to manage conflict effectively can help you maintain a healthy relationship. Fulfilling relationships involve two conscious people that are able to find solutions not only for the long recurring problems they face, but also for any unexpected challenges.

Relationships are not going to be linear, they are complex, yet simple. There are challenges in life that simply can't be overcome. However, with flexibility and awareness, any changes can be handled successfully.

Conscious partners address challenges with curiosity, allowing changes rather than resisting them. And when you accept challenges, they dissolve by themselves.

Changes and challenges are part of any relationship and without them the relationship cannot progress. They offer you a great opportunity to understand different perspectives, enrich your relationship and deepen mutual connection.

Staying connected with your partner is not an end stage, but a continuous process of growth and change. Deep connection is one of the greatest gifts you can offer to a relationship. It is experiencing love at an elevated level and truly thrive in your life.

Your relationship is going to be a transformative journey that will eventually change you in your in the most healed, loved, joyful and creative version of yourself.

Key takeaways

There is no perfect relationship. You are going to have the relationship you create, you develop, and you accept. Fulfilling relationships are complex, yet simple. They require two partners a little bit more conscious, a little bit more available, little bit more flexible and a little bit more healed. This little bit here and there has the potential to open a doorway to a more abundant, joyful, creative, and loving journey through life.

Bibliography

Becker-Phelps, Leslie, *Insecure in Love: How Anxious Attachment Can Make You Feel Jealous, Needy, and Worried and What You Can Do About It*. Oakland, CA, New Harbinger Publications, 2014.

Bowlby, J. *Attachment and Loss: Volume 1. Attachment*, New York, Basic Books, 1969.

Brown, Brené, The Gifts of Imperfection: Let Go of Who You Think You're Supposed to Be and Embrace Who You Are, 2010.

Chapman, Gary D., 1938, *The 5 Love Languages: The Secret to Love that Lasts*. Chicago: Northfield Publishing, 2015.

David, Susan A. *Emotional Agility: Get Unstuck, Embrace Change, and Thrive in Work and Life*. New York, Avery an imprint of Penguin Random House, 2016.

Dweck, C. S. *Mindset: The new psychology of success*. Random House, 2006.

Gabor, Maté. *When the Body Says No: The Cost of Hidden Stress*. Penguin Random House, 2019.

García, Héctor, et al. *Ikigai: The Japanese Secret to a Long and Happy Life*. Large print edition. Waterville, Maine, Thorndike Press Large Print, 2018.

Goleman, Daniel, *Emotional Intelligence*. New York, Bantam Books, 1995.

Gottman, J. M., & Gottman, J. S. Gottman couple therapy. In A. S. Gurman, J. L. Lebow, & D. K. Snyder (Eds.), *Clinical handbook of couple therapy* (5th ed., pp. 129–157). The Guilford Press, 2015.

Gottman, J. M., & Silver, N. The seven principles for making marriage work. [Pbk. ed.]. New York, Three Rivers Press, 2000.

Gray, John. *Men Are from Mars, Women Are from Venus: a Practical Guide for Improving Communication and Getting What You Want in Your Relationships. New York: HarperCollins, 1992.*

Harari, Yuval N., and Derek Perkins. *Sapiens: A Brief History of Humankind.* Unabridged. [Old Saybrook, Ct.], Tantor Media, Inc, 2015.

Johnson, Susan M. *Hold Me Tight: Seven Conversations for a Lifetime of Love.* New York, Little, Brown & Co, 2008.

Levine, P. A., & Frederick, A. *Waking the tiger: healing trauma: the innate capacity to transform overwhelming experiences.* Berkeley, CA: North Atlantic Books, 1997.

Pease, Allan. and Barbara Pease. *The Definitive Book of Body Language.* Bantam hardcover ed. New York, Bantam Books, 2006.

Perry, Bruce D. 1955- and Oprah, Winfrey, *What Happened to You?: Conversations On Trauma, Resilience, and Healing.* [New York], Macmillan Audio, 2021.

Robbins, Anthony. *Awaken the Giant Within: How to Take Immediate Control of Your*

Mental, Emotional, Physical & Financial Destiny. Pocket Books, 2001.

Rosenberg, Marshall B. *Nonviolent Communication: A Language of Life.* 2nd ed. Encinitas, CA, Puddle Dancer Press, 2003.

Tolle, Eckhart. *The Power of Now: A Guide to Spiritual Enlightenment.* Novato, California, New World Library, 1999.

Van der Kolk, Bessel A. *The Body Keeps the Score: Brain, Mind, and Body in the Healing of Trauma.* New York, New York, Penguin Books, 2015.

Made in the USA
Columbia, SC
26 August 2025

61742303R00065